GOD MADE SPACE

GOD MADE SPACE is part of the "God Made" series produced in collaboration with The Faraday Institute for Science and Religion.

Other titles in the series:

GOD MADE THE WORLD
GOD MADE ANIMALS

ABOUT THE AUTHORS

Steph Bryant loves animals, exploring, and enjoying nature. She became a wholehearted Christian while studying science at Cambridge University, when she began to realise that the wonder she felt in exploring science was really an invitation to worship God. Steph is passionate about looking after the world God has entrusted us with and, after working in conservation science, chose to spend her time helping young people explore the wonder of God's creation and our responsibility to care for it well.

Lizzie Henderson grew up loving God and exploring His creation through science. She is fascinated by the processes God uses to bring about creation's amazing diversity, and loves to encourage young people to find wonder in exploring what God has made. Since studying science at Cambridge University, Lizzie has been busy developing The Faraday Institute's Youth and Schools Programme, helping thousands of young people to explore their questions about science, faith, and our understanding of the universe.

Steph and Lizzie are the Youth and Schools Programme Co-Directors at The Faraday Institute for Science and Religion.

ABOUT THE PROJECT

The Faraday Institute for Science and Religion

The Faraday Institute is an interdisciplinary research and communication enterprise linked to the University of Cambridge. Our Youth and Schools Team are committed to providing high-quality events and resources that encourage young people of all ages and backgrounds to explore their questions about the interactions of science and religious faith in exciting and engaging ways.

If you and your children have enjoyed reading about how "God made space", why not explore more about science, faith, and what God has made at **www.faradaykids.com.** You'll find activities, videos, age-specific answers to common questions, and more about our other resources. You can also share your experience of reading this book with us!

Or check out **www.faradayeducators.com** for information about resources and events for parents, teachers, and other educators.

Faraday Kids Science and Religion

Faraday Educators Science and Religion Resources for Kids & Teens

This project and publication was made possible through the support of a grant from the John Templeton Foundation. The opinions expressed in this publication are those of the authors and do not necessarily reflect the views of the John Templeton Foundation.

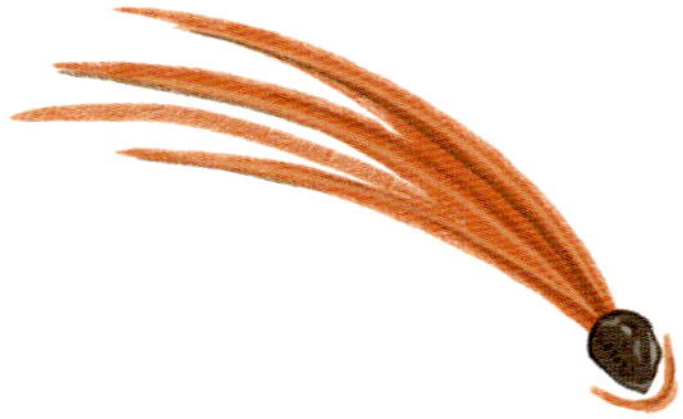

Illustrated by Steph Marshall

Published by
Lion Hudson Limited
Wilkinson House, Jordan Hill Business Park
Banbury Road, Oxford OX2 8DR, England

www.lionhudson.com

ISBN 978 0 7459 7783 6

First edition 2020

Acknowledgments: Scripture quotations taken from the ESV® Bible (The Holy Bible, English Standard Version®), copyright © 2001 by Crossway Bibles, a publishing ministry of Good News Publishers. Used by permission. All rights reserved.

A catalogue record for this book is available from the British Library

Printed and bound in China, October 2019, LH54

GOD MADE SPACE

Steph Bryant and Lizzie Henderson

Illustrated by Steph Marshall

LION CHILDREN'S

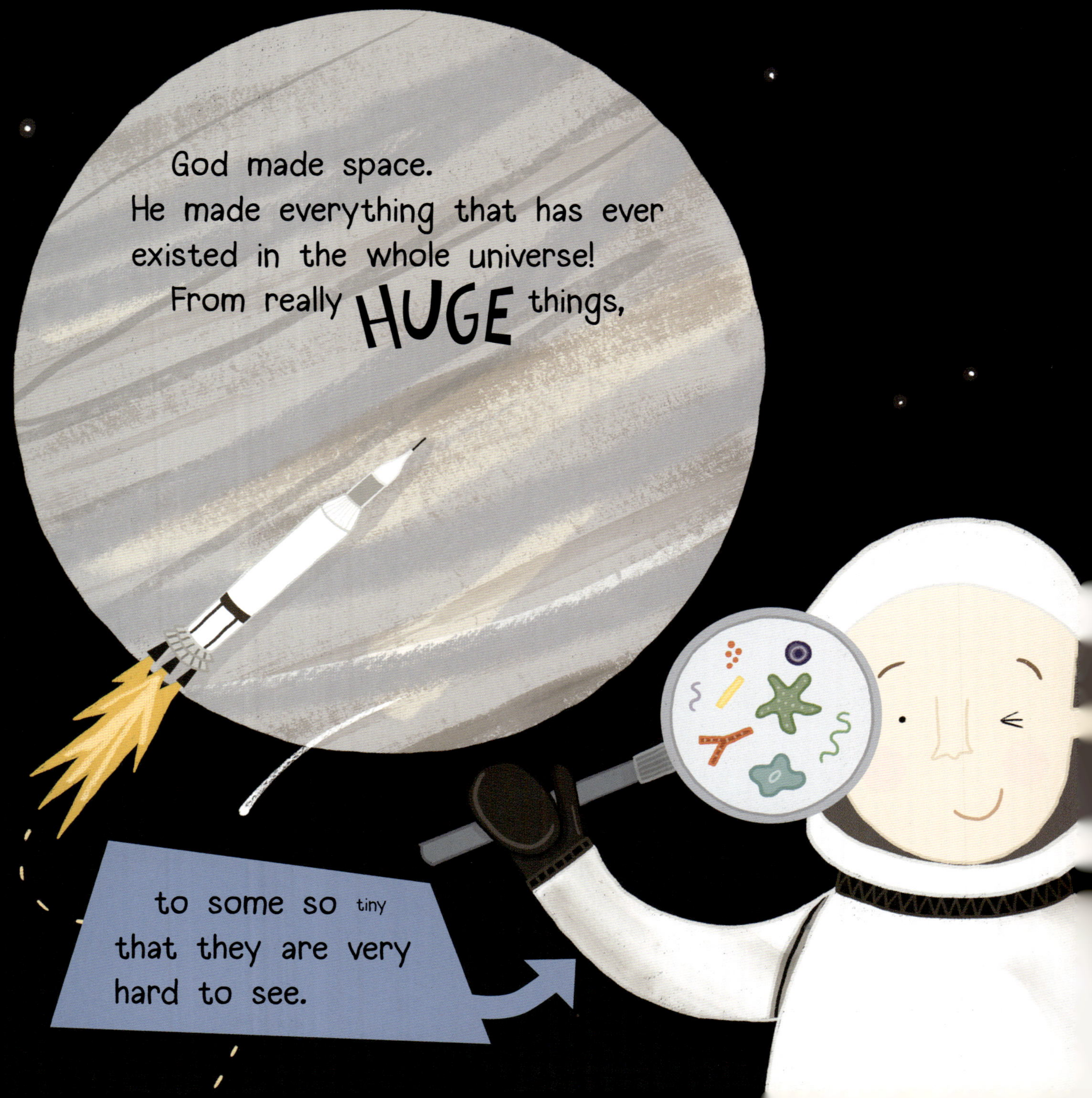

God made space.
He made everything that has ever existed in the whole universe!
From really **HUGE** things,

to some so tiny that they are very hard to see.

God has given us lots of clues about **HOW** He made space.

This is how we think He did it.

Before there was anything, there was nothing. Nothing at all. Apart from God. Then God made space. He started with a

HUGE EXPLOSION!

We call it the Big Bang. From a tiny beginning, space grew bigger and **bigger** and **bigger.**

God's universe is still growing today.

The first things in God's universe were tiny bits called particles. They were made in the huge explosion.

Over a long, long time, God has been using these particles to fill His universe with amazing things.

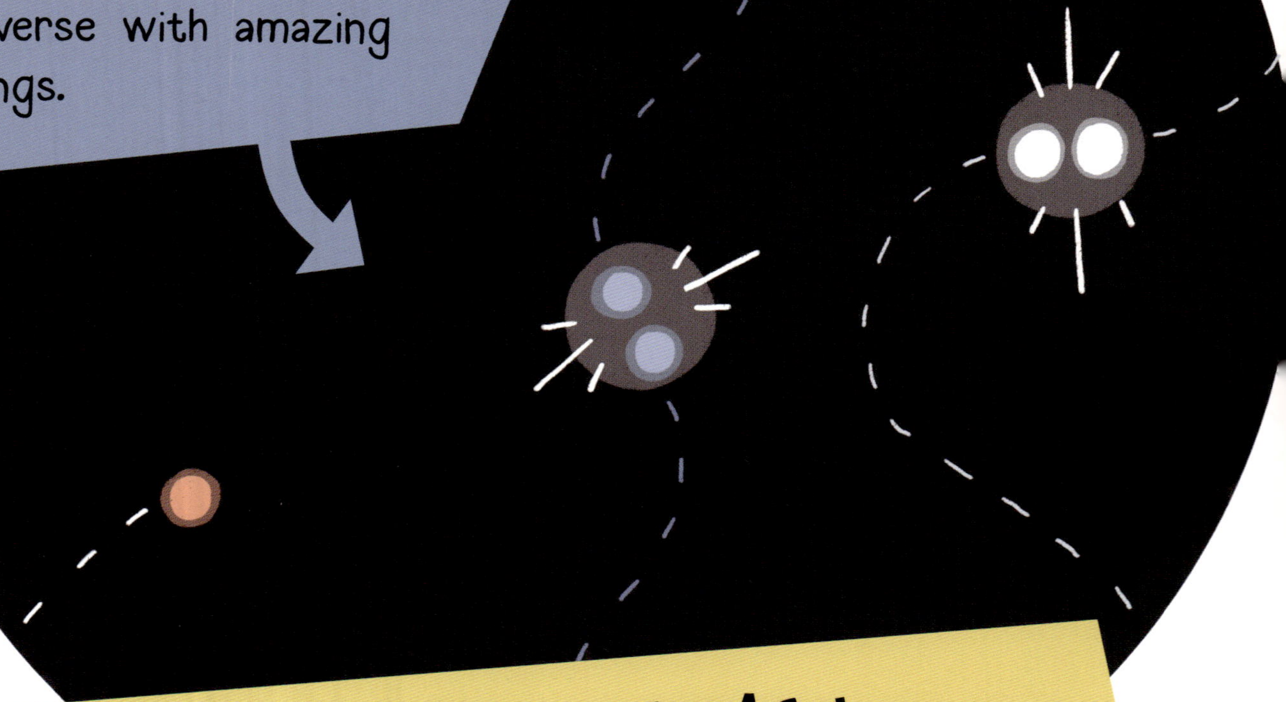

The particles **WHIZZ** and **CRASH** together,

building up into **HUGE** dusty clouds. God uses these clouds to make the stars, even today.

Stars are amazing. They sparkle and shine because they are very, very hot, like enormous bonfires!

There are so many stars –

MILLIONS and BILLIONS!

You could spend your whole life counting stars and still not count them all!

Telescopes are like special cameras that help us see things that are very far away. They show us that stars swirl around in huge, beautiful groups called galaxies.

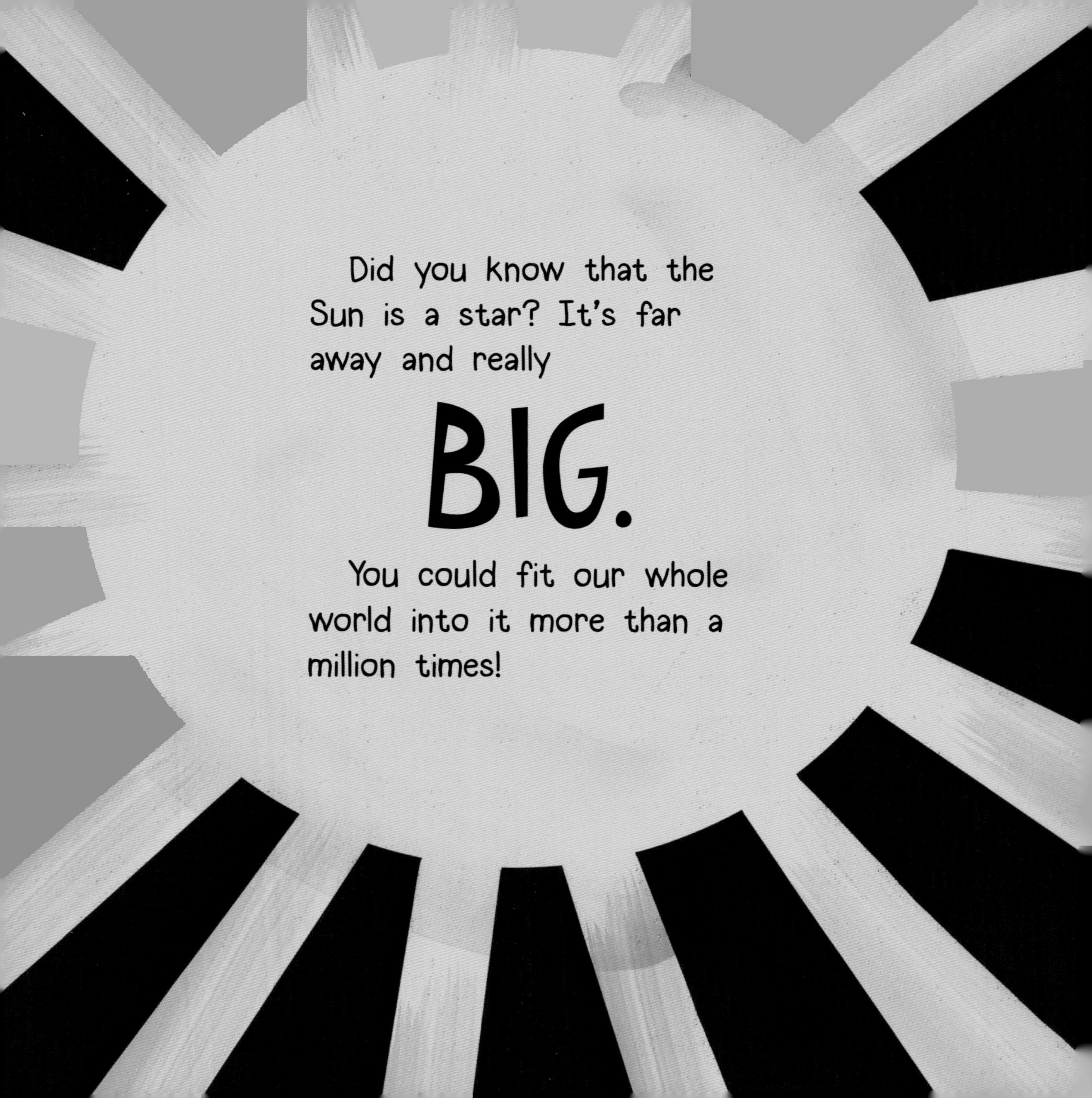

Did you know that the Sun is a star? It's far away and really

BIG.

You could fit our whole world into it more than a million times!

The Sun is so hot and bright that it makes all the light and warmth we need.

God's super-hot stars do something very important.

They squash and **squish** tiny particles together into new, **bigger** bits of stuff.

When stars get really, really old they can

EXPLODE!

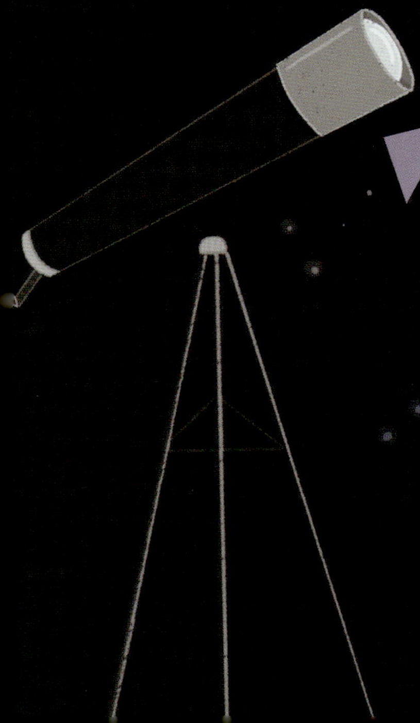

This happens very far away, but telescopes help us see all the bits inside whooshing out into space like enormous, beautiful fireworks.

God uses the bits of stuff made in stars like building blocks, to make everything else in the universe.

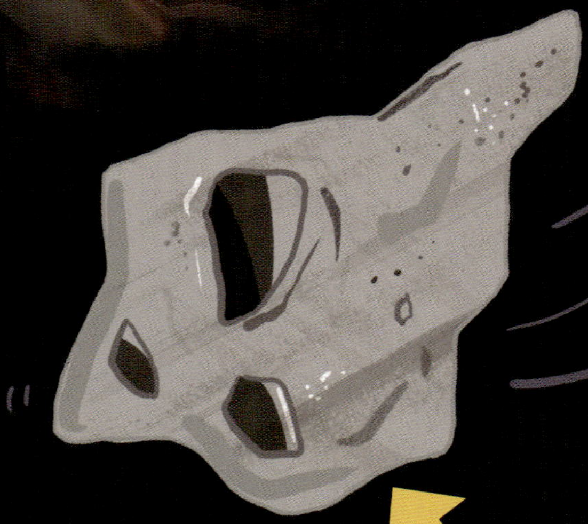

From huge rocky asteroids and icy comets that zoom around in space,

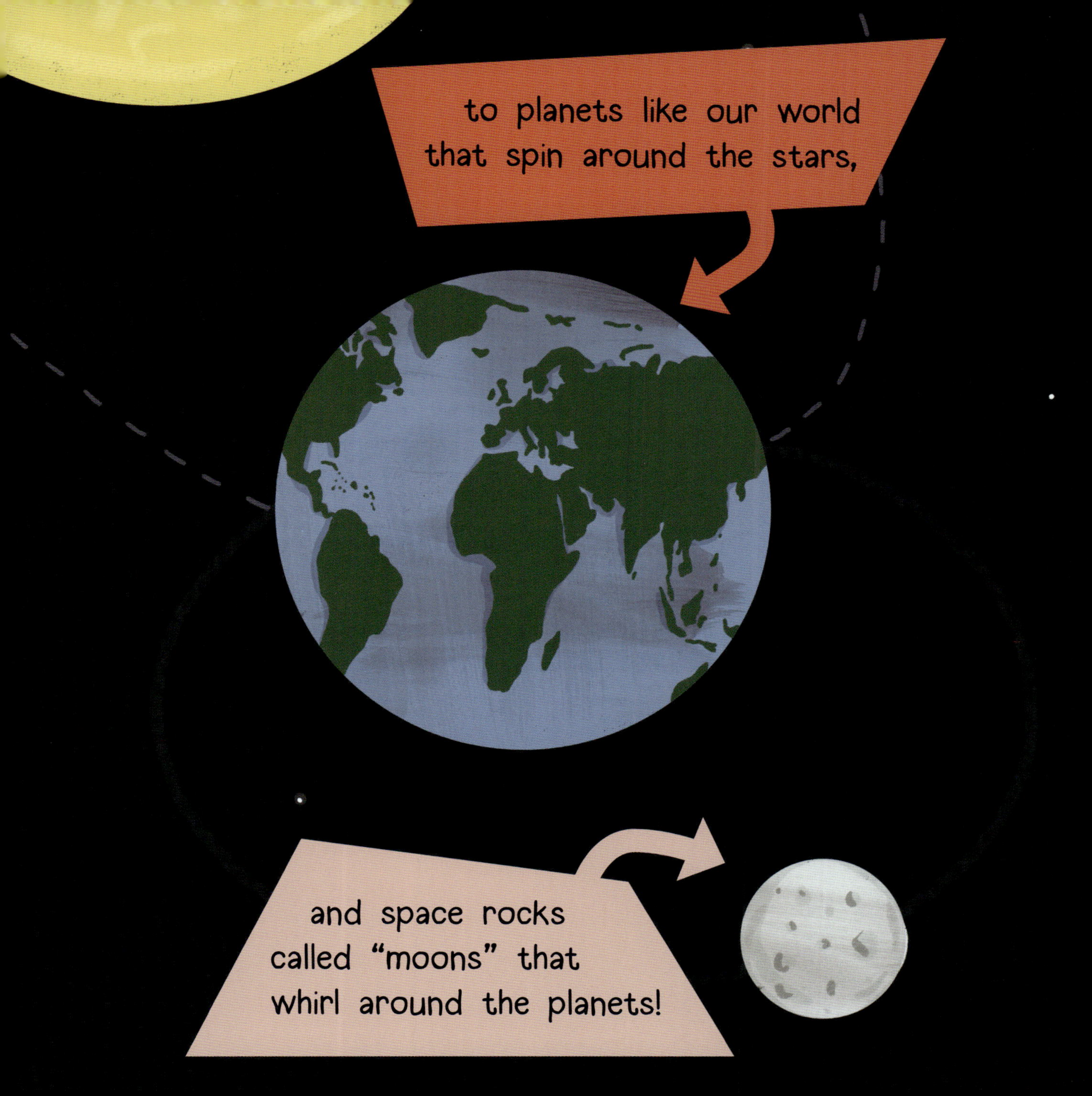
to planets like our world that spin around the stars,
and space rocks called "moons" that whirl around the planets!

God has made millions and billions of planets.

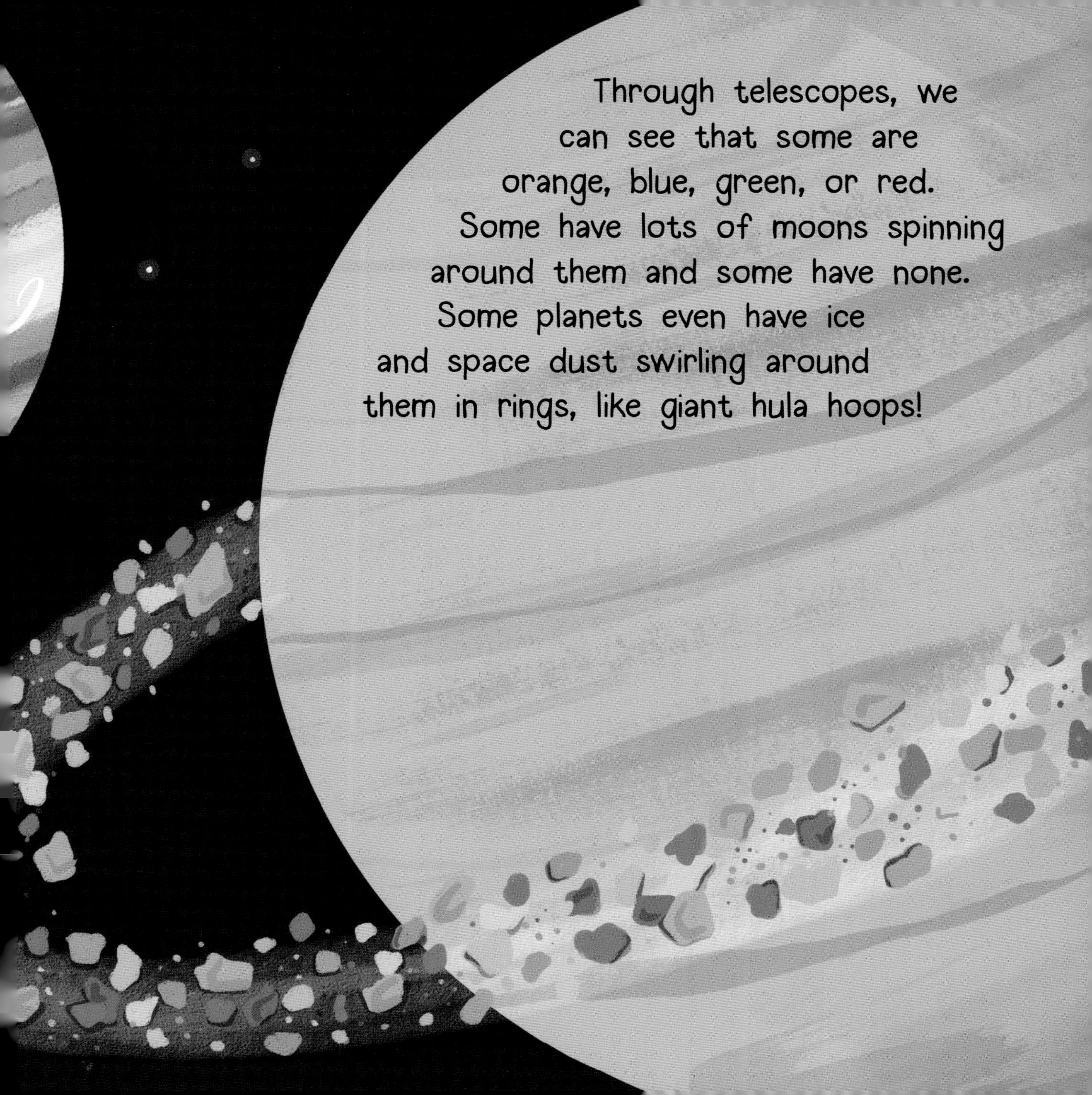

Through telescopes, we can see that some are orange, blue, green, or red. Some have lots of moons spinning around them and some have none. Some planets even have ice and space dust swirling around them in rings, like giant hula hoops!

It would be amazing to explore other planets up close. But God's universe is **HUGE** and other planets are so far away that even speedy rockets would take many months to reach the nearest one, called Mars!

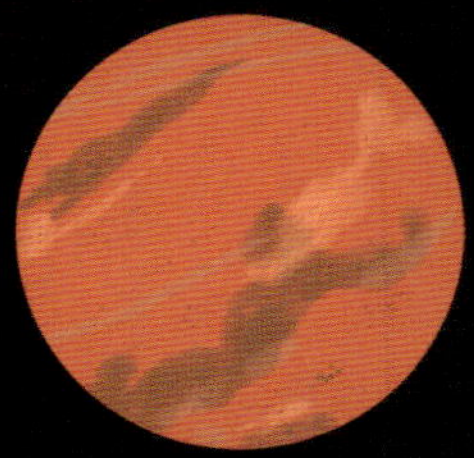

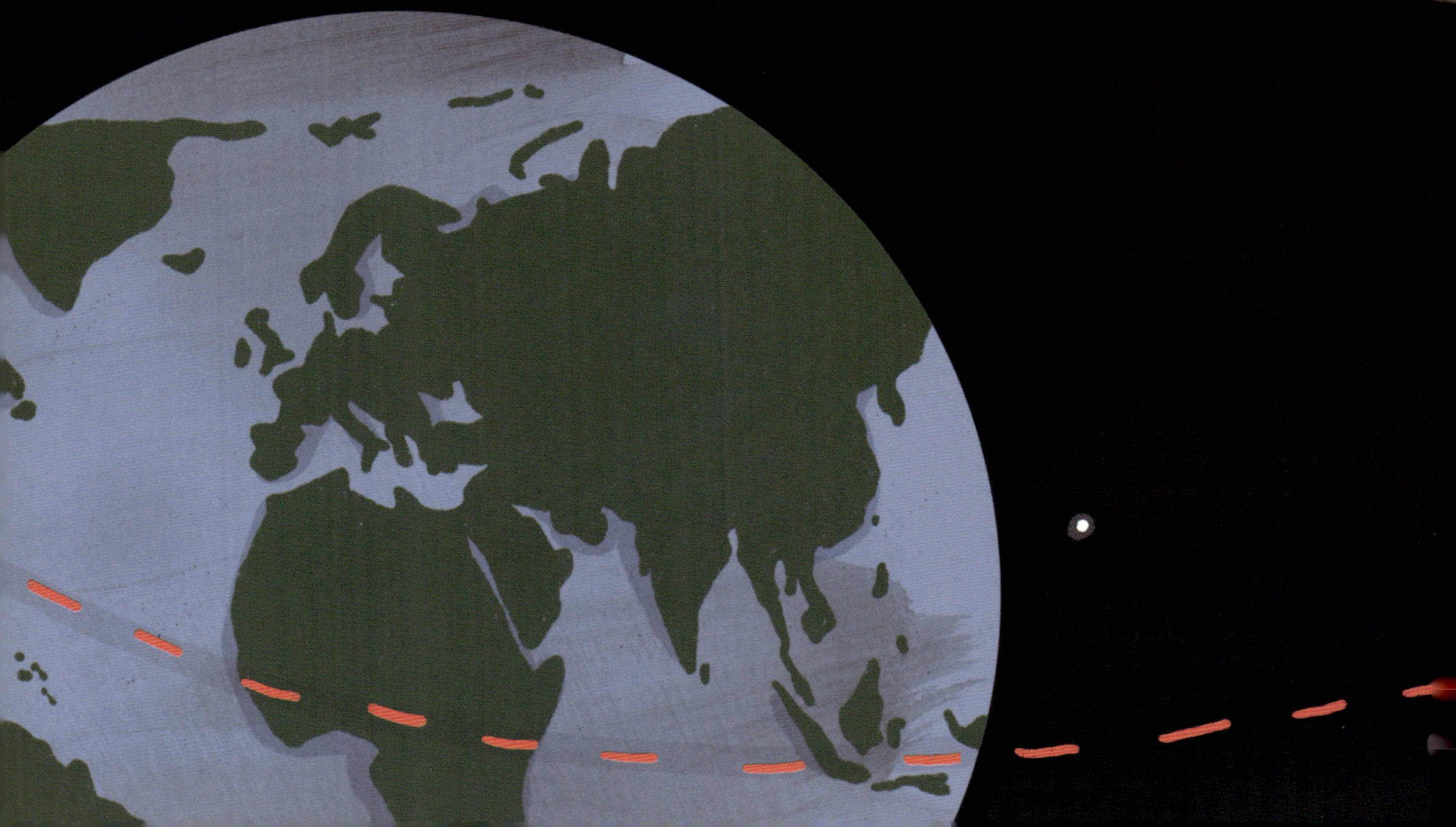

Our moon is closer. A rocket trip to the Moon takes about three days. But it would take months to get to the Sun, and to get to the next nearest star would take around 80,000 years!

God loves it when we learn about the things He has made! From His stars and starry building blocks, to everything made from them –

asteroids,

comets,

moons,

planets like
our world and
everything on it,
all zooming and
spinning around in space!

People have invented things like telescopes, rockets, and robots, which help us to explore more of God's **BRILLIANT** universe.

Maybe one day you'll go into space and see for yourself?

God has made an amazing universe, and He loves everything He has made.

EXPERIMENTS AND ACTIVITIES

Why not try out these fun activities to help your little ones think a bit more about the amazing universe God has made? You can find some helpful hints and tips at www.faradaykids.com/activities.

STAR SPOTTING

How does it make you feel when you look at God's amazing creation? Head outside on a clear dark afternoon or evening and see if you can spot the moon, some stars or even planets!

PAINT THE NIGHT SKY

Get thinking about the millions and billions of stars God has made by painting a glittery night sky full of sparkles.

PLANET ART

Get creative with fun shaving foam paintings and think about God's creativity in making all the different kinds and colours of planets.

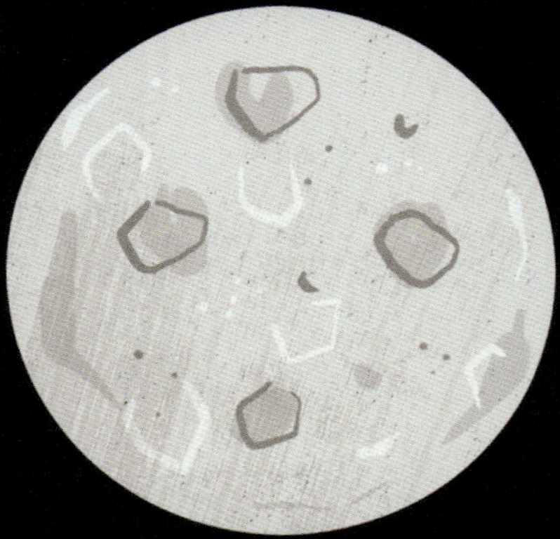

SPACE PLAYDOUGH

Consider God's love for His creation as you imagine your own galaxies with a creative playdough universe activity.

MAKE YOUR OWN ROCKET

Use your own science skills and see the amazing things science helps us understand about God's universe by sending a bubble-powered rocket flying up into the sky.

A NOTE ABOUT SCIENCE AND THE BIBLE

As humans, we love to question, explore, and discover the world around us, and our place in it. *God Made Space* is written to help even the youngest humans begin to explore the universe God made them to be a part of.

***God Made Space* gives an inviting overview of mainstream scientific ideas about how the universe works. It celebrates the glimpse that science offers into God as creator, and the way our wonder can increase as we find out more about His universe.**

Almost every book of the Bible talks about God as creator and His relationship with creation. The more we understand about who wrote each part of the Bible – when, why, and for whom – the more we can enjoy what they tell us about God.

The Bible doesn't discuss every part of God's creation. Dinosaurs, general relativity, black holes, bacteria, pandas or penguins don't get a look in! But this doesn't mean the Bible is inaccurate or outdated. Rather than talking about atomic structure or the speed of light thousands of years before people were asking questions about them, God led the authors to focus on His power, love, and authority in ways that were relevant and radical at the time, and still are today.

The Bible is full of people marvelling at the expanse of the stars, the beauty of God's creatures, and the processes of nature – seeing God's glory in it all.

***"The heavens declare the glory of God"* (Psalm 19:1)**

***"Great are the works of the Lord, studied by all who delight in them."* (Psalm 111:2)**

Today, all over the world, people are still drawn to worship God through exploring the expanse, depth, and intricacies of His creation. From the youngest child to the world's top scientists, God delights in our wonder at His creation.

"I believe God gave us intelligence so that we could investigate and appreciate the wonders of His creation."

Francis Collins
Geneticist

"We are free to explore the universe with joyful curiosity, relying on God's faithfulness, discovering all the wonderful 'hows' and 'whens' of creation, about which scripture tells us 'who' and 'why'."

Deborah Haarsma
Astrophysicist

We hope that *God Made Space* will encourage you and your little ones to share in God's delight by exploring the creation He loves and experiencing wonder, awe, and worship for yourselves. To explore further, check out our other books or head to our website: **www.faradaykids.com.**